gravity loves the body

monika lee

Library and Archives Canada Cataloguing in Publication

Lee, Monika, 1962-

gravity loves the body / Monika Lee.

Poems.
ISBN 978-0-919139-06-0

I. South Western Ontario Poetry (Firm) II. Title.

PS8623.E32G773 2008   C811'.6   C2008-904829-6

South Western Ontario Poetry
London, Ontario

This book is dedicated with love and gratitude to my father, Alvin A. Lee.

Acknowledgements

I extend my sincere thanks to the literary presses and editors who first published many of these poems, some in a slightly different form.

EBIP (formerly HMS Press) and the Canadian Poetry Association (London Chapter), under the editorship of Wayne Ray, published "the woman with the empty bowl," "a mother's dying," and "ninth month" in my chapbook, *slender threads* (2004).
"listen" first appeared in *Dalhousie Review*.
"country," "spring" and "prophecy: 2" in *The Nashwaak Review*.
"blake 445f" in *Harpweaver* (where it won the Canadian Authors' Association Joan Tovenati Memorial Award for poetry).
"the woman with the empty bowl" in *Antigonish Review*.
"marrakech" in *Prairie Journal*.
"a play" in *Ottawa Arts Review: The University of Ottawa's Comprehensive Literary and Arts Journal*.
"minutiae" and "mother's closet" in *Room of One's Own: Celebrating the Best in Women's Literature*.
"thea" and "the bathers" in *Quills: Canadian Poetry Magazine*.
"earthbound" in *Atlantis: A Women's Studies Journal*.
"tangible words" in *Event: The Douglas College Review*.
"ice shards and blade marks" in *The Fiddlehead*.
"mother as poet," and "living room" in *The Madwoman in the Academy: 43 Women Boldly Take on the Ivory Tower*.
"ninth month" in *Qwerty*.
"sun, pines and prophecy" in *Canadian Woman Studies: les cahiers de la femme*.
"doll hospital," in *Tower Poetry*.
"a mother's dying" in *Canadian Literature*.
"indwelling" in *Strong Winds*.
"julian the magician" in *Afterthoughts*.

Cover design by Ann Mayer

I am deeply grateful to Olive Senior for her insight, editing, and encouragement. I thank the Humber College School of Writing for awarding me a "letter of distinction" and nominating me for the 2007 North American Best New Poets Anthology.

I gratefully acknowledge James Doelman, Dominick Grace, Lorna Bowman, Theresa Topic, and Brescia University College for ongoing creative support. My thanks are also given to Susan Merskey, Sheila Martindale and Brenda Alden for their hard work and commitment, and to Ann Mayer for both friendship and artistic advice.

I appreciate and thank especially Brian Diemert, to whom these poems owe genesis and incarnation, and our loving and inspiring daughters, Anna and Natasha Lee-Diemert. A profound thank you to Dad, for all. Only you know how much that is.

contents

offerings

ninth month	13
mother as poet	14
mantra	15
the bathers	16
living room	17
child on jebel toubkal	18
our weather	19
middle cove	20
ducks	21
girls	22

lapsarian

because	25
the obscurity of you	26
undreamed	27
repairs	28
farewell	29
accident	30
morning goodbye	32
bone dry	33
descent	34
memory	36
the last time	37
lapsarian	39
laughter and midnight	40

taken

doll hospital	43
chickens	44

circumventing death 45
a mother's dying 46
mother's closet 47
home from work 48
hrothgar 50
lie 51
minutiae 52
elegy 53
choreography 54
visions 56

earth

mammal 59
a play 60
spring 61
black-eyed susans 62
ice shards and blade marks 63
thea 64
wind 65
country 66
serpent 67
north 68
perversity 69
floorboards 70

oracles

indwelling 73
marrakech 74
majorelle garden 75
southern oases 76
riad dar fakir 77
mhamid 79
sacred 80
sahara 81

prophecy: 2   82
sun, pines and prophecy   83
time   84
to julian the magician   85
chinese restaurant   86
votive candles in cathedrals   87
the woman with the empty bowl   88

word

earthbound   91
listen   92
ineffable   93
tin drums   94
spatial poetics and the message of the pebble   95
tangible words   96
activist shopping   97
blake 445f   98
bog poem   100
writing   101

offerings

ninth month

my shell is brittle now and drier by the day,
but you will crack me open
and the pain will leave no bruises,
searing with the flow of yolk,

a solar gelatin.

i have resisted,
denied the ball-hard force of being.

soon to be subsumed by virgin anguish,
my eggshell flesh is steady though trembling:
pearl-bright and diaphanous,
a cloud your light will scatter.

mother as poet

i dedicate myself to the preservation of our love,
even though i sit, pores clogged
with scraps of ibm and dust,
so adverse to the tactile brightness of your shine,

once submerged in a oneness so vital to our being,
now propped and dangling on the knees of learning,
straining for a dagger-hewn piece of action,
separating me . . . oh, aching . . .from wordless,
infant.

understand that these are the words and weeds
that form the garden of my psyche.
without them i am no more me,
than are you you without chunky thighs
and seventeen solid and delectable pounds.

mantra

hunger and its language are human.
meaning, or hunger sated, is mammary.

when matrix becomes mother,
longing hooks onto a nipple
in skin-touch
or animate pillow.

milk transduces a margaric babe
into a child of honey.

for mama, body speaks well,
and pours this over-ripened fruit
into a moon-shaped mouth,

a flesh-mantra
succulent.

the bathers

skin to skin in tepid water
murky with soap and milk,
your body distends across an abdominal island.

we are the petals of one flower,
we are silk and velvet woven together:
marine creatures dwelling
in a country of air.

in your mouth "mirror" sounds like "me your."
a dolphin slips against a mossy matrix

with eyes of awe and shining,
cheek pressed like pearl against my oyster breast;

a moment of aquatic wonder
floating beneath the curtain,
a breath and stillness
as pliant as you.

to be mother-of-pearl
the silence of promise.

living room

let those who choose to, run the world,
while i fathom and breathe small rushes of joy.

(in any case)
poems cannot be written in
a windowless computer room,

here verse flows plainly across an untidy shag,
threads its way through the
                        tangled rocking horse mane
and over the crumpled flannelette cows.

garlic skins, bespeaking a creative presence,
have fallen confetti-like in our midst,
while the antique horse (bless him)
has no use for oats,
and the toy kitchen no need for plumbing.

child on jebel toubkal

solo she walks beyond the forest wall,
leaps across the void, flying.
there is no silence like still air.

above the granite cliffs she soars
and we can only watch her trembling
blue grey wings of ether,
bright red streaks of sunset against her form.

she falls forward into freedom
with a dancer's arch and smile.

and she is not yours or mine,
nor is she even with us –
her dwelling-place is not home.

our weather

giggles and squeals behind the chair,
shafts of sunlight on bobbing heads –
together beam and shine play on
a duo of sound,
a sound of light.

but weather is sudden on domestic coasts
when a warm front (chuckler and toy thief)
meets a cold gale (it's her sister's)
there is trouble times two, tempest and quake,
thrown back to primal rage
followed by an embrace.

wild curls like filaments of breeze,
laughing eyes and tiny toes spill into the room.
vigorous pratfalls, plosive offerings –
they are summer air.

middle cove

we build a zen garden from coloured stones;
my job is to keep the stones wet and shiny

and hers is to run back and forth
with stones and water

dancing and laughing
water and stones

stones under water
water over stones.

she carries the large ones
and i fear for her bones.

she says she'll cover the whole beach with water,
this daughter
of salt water and stones.

ducks

a dozen ducklings chase the falling stars
dropping on the water.
the stars are unextinguished
but tremble across the lake.

the mother duck is chasing a dog,
she squawks and bursts while
the retriever, born and bred to hunt,
is scared away.

sunlight follows the mother and her young,
she keeps the dog from her downy ones.
sun spangles follow birds and
light bouncing on the waves.

girls

little girls are spring birds,
twirling and tossing in their nest.
they are so right the eye
cannot believe its luck
to land on those rare feathers.

a cheek is so soft
i cannot free myself from its touch.
i cannot love all of life because you
are too much glory for time.

lilac and clover lure bees
around the raspberry canes.
each time a buzz dollops the ear
we sense fruition:
nectar turned to honey,
love turned to children,
breath into word.

lapsarian

because

because i love you
i eat apples instead of berries.

because i need you
i give our books away.

because i have you
i wake the neighbours weeping.

because i'm near you
i go to distant lands.

because i know you
i paint your face in colours.

because i touch you
i sing your body white.

because i want you
i serve food in clay dishes.

because i envy you
i watch the setting sun.

because i hold you
the night is never long.

the obscurity of you

you are not nearly. i imagine. the reality is something
other than the shards of meaning. splits of language.
space present and undefiled. time in a cup. curls
tossed in a pile like the heap of mixed-up thoughts of
you that in my mind crowd out all things of use. like
smoke coming off the bonfires in the spring. casting an
ominous blanket here and there across the wide river
flats. the light grey clay. the sandy washed-away acres
on the banks. dark not brilliant in the stormy weather.
you not you, but obscure half-reference to the contents
of my mind. a brain transplant. lulled hypnotized
half-dreaming half-awake. into a nether zone of
spilling. in the twilight of my vulva. in the darkness of
my smooth canal. you inhabit these dark places.
these spots of violent integration. unknowing. unbeing.
not fully or even you.

undreamed

wearing your shirt at night
has not helped me dream the dream
we long for, two halves
of one apple, fallen,
not yet bitten.

saying your name at night
did not unloose the binding sheets
of dream-cocoon, of sleep
that held me,
pinned down the lost dream
still and alone undreamed.

reading your letter at night
so funny, true and pained,
as my head fell on the
pillow, body on sheet, sweat
on the chill of night
did not unloose, unpin
the dream of you.

and still each night
the same song plays across
my ears, no dream or image
on the blank, razed screen, but
words incarnate, apple halves unbit,
song's mere sound
to reach for you still
undreamed.

repairs

peeling paint and broken door hinges,
visible signs of our failure to build a theory,
do not bother you at all,
do not threaten the parameters of your thinking,
or break the codes of mine.

we are perversely fond of crumbling,
of picking apart the pieces of cheese
in jigsaw form or tearing bits of shortbread
dropping it in the gaps of floorboards.
this process is debilitating but essential
to the sipping slippery hungering throat;

repairs are not only costly and irritating,
they cramp our cool loser style.
they're completely out of line with
the inner gulf – water, like words, pours
through these cracks in the drywall ruins
and we have need of this.

farewell

there is no way to admit our past
and still touch the skin of this child.

our unborn child is the aching of the days,
the memory of elm leaves and horizon

falling cataracts behind the sounds.
our unbegotten children are vibrations in the air;

they spin away from me.

nostalgia for the trouble you caused,
striving for your retinal light –

sad eyes with blinding light
searching orbs so sadly bright.

our child is the isolated spirit
you heap earth on and bury

with no stone or epitaph, no sigh
or song, other than this sound.

accident

i took a mean swerve and
skidded off the highway of today
right at the start:

woke late with someone's headache,
checked e-mail fifteen times;
forgot my morning bathe.

i realized i chose the wrong novel,
stepped in chicken poo,
listened to complaints about michael jackson.

forgot to eat a lunch,
forgot to write a poem,
forgot to collapse in grief.

i did remember to
consult the tarot for the 93rd time
about why you left,

but did not send that card,
return the neighbour's mail
or post a cheque to unicef for rehydration pills,

nor did i collect the eggs,
fondle my secret spot,
or speak of all my love.

i skidded into the ditch of today
and stayed immobilized
awaiting roadside help,

unfeeling and unmoving,
i stared into untravelled distances
wondering what might have been.

morning goodbye

your flesh coaxes sweetness from the room and its
         fabrics.
you leave the possible woman for disturbed air and
         bungling,
the outer world with its stain of derogation, its absence
         of touch
the meetings, answerings, readyings, and memos
         of urgency.

abandonment of love

love is as easy as falling from a log
the one hard thing
surrender.

bone dry

the last owners of this place
lost a son to brain damage –
there is no water and
none of the doors work.
a drought last summer made pines and
bushes wither, and the toilets could not be flushed.
the children went to school with dirty hair.

we knew all along
there was water deep down
and we waited four months
for the well to be dug.

the diviners finally came
and dug up the lawn.
the well is there now;
it gives ten gallons a minute,
they said, and left without hooking it up.

perhaps
if we remove the dead trees
and fix the broken doors,

perhaps
if we love a little harder
and pray a little more,

perhaps
the water will come
to the damaged

and bring to parched lips and empty holes
a moistening.

descent

consider this garden
the grand measure
of my illusions,

its weedy chaos,
an untimely
descent

into the
vining bloom of
underworld spores.

churned up
clumps of passion
are compost.

whoever created the notion
of stability
or comfort

knew nothing of this mess
in the ground,
this root cellar,

knew nothing of abduction
imprisonment
or coma,

choked blossoms
of the descent
whispering across

the stranglehold of weeds
broken pomegranate
fading melody

for this garden
we steal water
from the river,

as though love were
not meagre or moribund,
but living
underneath.

memory

purity of birth
as obliteration;
the smallest stone
tumbles from the eaves
of starkness
into the blackened pool
of yesterday.

nothing is clear,
not your voice or name
sinking past memory
sphinx of this cargo,
its untellable journey,
the birthing of stones.

the last time

in the car you were so close,
i might have touched your hair,

messy curls waving goodbye
to many somewheres.

you wanted to meet again,
but i stared wordless at the car floor.

you left a book,
token of return,

you left music,
someone later stole.

you said someday
you'd show your poems,

but you were going away
to someone or to someones.

later that night someone
held on to me so tight

i didn't mind your leaving,
but the heart suffers hairline fractures.

i wish now i'd touched those curls,
driven slower, gone home later,

gone inside your house or mind,
prolonged the moment

spent it to the farthing for
someone now gone somewhere.

lapsarian

the garden had not walls
beyond the concrete
no

that impermeable
negative.

we ate well,
loved serenely;
we played with the
lions and leopards.

but no loomed
sound or shadow
on our bliss, a phantom sun;

it echoed to us
our name, our place
of loss.

laughter and midnight

this was a room of love.
do not be deceived by its beige walls,
antiseptic corners and pristine silence.

this room is in denial.
true, there are no birthday cards
or children's paintings stuffed in drawers,
but children painted here
and snuggled in the monolithic bed.

no smudgy ring or sticky soap allows
anyone soaked in its tub with laughter and midnight.
no shelves exist with well-pressed flowers
in pages of old books,
yet heaney's poems were read aloud
by lovers in the night.

not a single photo has been taped on the mirror.

all the same,
in a house 300 miles away
snapshots of this room are clipped to several mirrors
and to a fridge with more than tiny booze bottles.

in this room
there are no panties on the floor or
rumpled sweat-filled sheets.
the scent of our bodies' cleft
has been bleached out.

still,
don't let the bleak conformist walls
and smooth grey bedspread fool you.
this was a room of love.

taken

doll hospital

whenever a doll lost a limb or eye
my clement tears fell
and i sent her to the doll hospital
gave her secret care –
more clothes, crisper blankets
the best.

when sister was born and i not walking
banged my head on the floor
whenever she nursed
no glassy eye fell from my china face
no leg was yanked ajar

the doll refuge stands awash
dream-solid and fragile as dice
oh, i tried so hard to hide from them
which ones i loved the best.

chickens

cold winds
and my father-in-law is dying,

pink blooms crumble,
rhode island reds
peck at them, chirping
loudly at the pane
large pink potted daisies
are floral chicken-feed.

natasha sheds tears for
plants that die.

they run, speckled, through long
grass, climb through holes in chicken
wire.

i hope the neighbour's dogs don't
eat them, because i'm not having more
babies, and the girls would cry,

as they will when grandpa dies,
the dead daisies testify.

circumventing death

the body is propped and powdered
to make believe it's him.
it could be the wrong one
so slight is the resemblance.

they cover it with flowers
and put it in a bed of silk.
his wife talks on and on
of who will mow the lawn.
one grandchild thinks the corpse is him.
one says he is an angel.

a third would like his poker chips,
but it's too soon to ask.

the truth is
a stale and hideous husk of useless flesh
is worse than nothing.

maybe he's somewhere having
a laugh at our futile gestures.

i see the look he'd have,
his rolled eyes, his spirit words,
"my, my."

a mother's dying

oral history:

my mother whispered to hers, "it's like childbirth,
you have to let go,"
as she slipped away from herself
leaving the body chill, dying is surely
one way of being born.

new reading:

it is akin to her own birth
for the child to behold a mother's dying

exegesis:

our history is sprinkled with the salt of loss
forfeiture defines the pair of us
and all our words have been an elegy
to that primordial unity
before weaning, school and weddings pulled me
from the anchor of your flesh.

a mother's dying is the final echo of being born.
birth was the first time i lost her
her death will be the last.

mother's closet

i wept hard for you:
harder than wire,
closer than fear,
a loss contained and uncontained.

no mother floats along the breeze,
rainbows still cross the speckled air,
image after image descends on me
until your very clothes become rainbows
pearl drops of atmosphere
crystallized into cloth,
the stuff of dreams worn on the body
outliving you
surpassing tender flesh.

home from work

the thing to do
is to pick up the mail,
sort the bills,
recycle the waste.

the thing to do
is to turn up the furnace;
walls and windows of
an old house bleed heat.

the thing to do
is to keep on my coat,
so the scratch, scratch
in my throat goes away.

the thing to do
is to feed the cat
before i trip and fall
on her shiny coat, thickened
from time alone
in this old, cold house,
and so she keeps it on,
as i should too.

the thing to do
is to make the tea,
to warm the scratch, scratch
of the throat, the cat and the window
tearing at the escaping minutes
which tick on the cold, mantle clock.

the thing to do
is not to think,
but scratch the throat of
the window with the mail,
cat mewing in the minutes
passing, escaped.

not to think of years passing,
parents newly dead or
passing into the cold, cold
scratching at the window,
recycling the waste,
we ought to bury them
wearing coats.

hrothgar

it isn't the violence i told them,
or the funereal aspect of our guest hall;
the shields of the fallen emblazon the walls,
and a hero from the gelts may save us.

even if nothing were rotten in denmark,
no monsters taking people in the night,
no weeping mothers or sighing widows,
there is something else –

the split and gravelly sound of the crows
tells the tale better than i,
the way the skin on my hand chaps and bleeds,
my silver ring against broken fingernails,

my impotence and kindliness
with wealtheow in the night,
a sense i've failed them all.

that all my thoughts and cares
should yield this crop of corpses.
like a blind horse in a corner i stand,
flies circle and land on my eyes.

hurry, beowulf, to my kindgom,
so i may swear a last oath,
my body rolled in a blanket like a child
sent to join and serve in heaven's hall
with the guests, our brethren revived.

lie

sometimes a lie is arrested in mid-flight
falls,
      feathers bloodied, to the earth.

we have the sight,
and courage to pull the trigger,

but when it squawks its last,
falling into an empty valley,

there's no triumph,
no garden of truth,
no peaceable kingdom,

just the rustle of leaves,
the brook over stones,

and recognition of what was meant,
a whiff of loss, a fleck of guilt.

captured or torn, it
leaves nothing to fill its echo.

minutiae

i give myself
to minutiae;
they get me from one day to the next
if barely

they are plain and simple and
undemanding.

dancing or painting or making a soul
takes energy.

i give myself
to banality.
what possible use is joy.

the time clock measures my circumference.
raging hate and love belong elsewhere.
i answer memos with devotion and care
the way monks say orisons
or buddhists their mantras.
discipline is the core of faith;
the edges of life should be neat and fastidious.

still, i marvel at their proximity.
the edges are so near.
i can just see across them.

last night a gardener came to my house
and identified all the plants.
he found hemlock by the door.
the door is an edge;
the hemlock just beyond it;
how thin the line between them.

elegy

dying is not beautiful.
falling, unraveling
you did not wish to go
but clung to shoes and floors,
to sitting up.

struggling to attach,
the body faltered,

you did not go gently.
some do not long to travel
across the sky,
but wish to stay with newspapers and children,
hockey games, barbecues,
and wife.

for some
to be a man sitting in a house
is more than heaven.

choreography

1

as a child at the ballet, i wondered aloud
why life was not more like the dance.
my father whispered his assent and mother
dressed me as giselle.

at home we shared the ballet *barre*
took our lessons together
in pubescence and menopause
thinness and obesity, in discipline,
exaltation, assumption, ascension.

no one told me a mother's body
would someday cease its dancing.

2

choreographer of a daughter's life,
i take anna to the oceanside where we lie
under gauzy white nets
wrapping the ocean-blue bed.

memories vexed me,
bothered and haunted the *grand pas d'action*
of moments not quite moments
of days not even lived
unsoldered *arabesques* and *portes de bras*
the unperformed *battements* of our limbs.

and so we ran to the shore
tore off our raiment
defied the cold of the spray

danced naked in the dionysian sea
with weeds and rocks wave-dancing too
singing beyond the white veils
effacing in moments
the nighttime of death and rebirth.

visions

curiosity powerful as wind,
like a fleet of mighty ships under sail,
pervades

a large cosmic kaleidoscope of
darkness and shining.

earth

mammal

the hum of flies around the eaves
diminishes solitude,
despite the natural estrangement
of insects and mammals.

mammal (mammalia)
is the mammary nomenclature
of our species –
we lost the true body
to gratify the false.

ma =
the heat in the blood,
muscles brimming with hot,
blood tending and spilling
into the brain like milk.

sympathy is mammalian,
and it's helpful to feel kin
to the flies,
buzzing though they are
and alien in the eaves.

a play

an infestation of benevolent bugs
on the window's inner pane,
they gather on-stage like an ensemble cast
in a postmodern musical comedy.

(off-stage actors supply music).
four ladybugs and five house flies perform
a minute and asymmetrically choreographed
exploration of the elevated stage –

they skirt dried raindrops,
specks of dirt and sticky sap.
sunlight shines from the other side
of the play – void of props and sets.

after two hours without pause,
the actors disperse, quitting
the audience (of one) with a drop-stained
stage of a face in lieu of applause.

spring

in these new days
joy is inconvenient.
celebration is a form of deviance
and gods are unwelcome guests.

and yet

flowers, violet and yellow,
burst forth from the mud
– the brown mess of dying in our garden
all autumn, winter – and now
the impudent blooms claim the barren spaces,
the eyes dilate to colour,
green edges outward,
past our eyes
into the temples;
the daffodil's trumpet of no tone
echoes its soundless notes into the air.

and joy is necessary,
the brown land recedes.

black-eyed susans

it disturbed me at first,
this unabashed indolence of the flowers,
their deviant lassitude.
with a black centre in their radiant faces,
they have a look of falling, but never drop;
nervy blooms to be so pendant
unbuttressed and unstaked.

ice shards and blade marks

this year the river threw up
foot-thick ice shards,
                    pancake-piled,
interlaced
                    with queen anne's faded blooms.
snow-covered marshmallows in milk.

footprints and tracks have
                    crisscrossed.
jet trails mimic
                    the tracks,
their thin clouds oppose the land.

untread snow yields to feet,
so i pushed on
fearing the ice beneath
would
        cave
            in,
                    and it did.

sprinkled ice floats on the brown river
as coconut in a curry
                    and the sun glares
like a watchful cook.

impromptu skating rinks
                    are hewn from the river bank,
tight with blade marks,
                    like jet trails,
crossed tracks,
                    and the shards of words.

thea

a bird saved from certain death, wing
broken at the road,
still and grey across the stones.

refuting the oracle, we save her
give her to a child – hands
picking and threading a nest of scars

twig bed of wounds.
she emits untameable tremblings
at our care, water, and seeds.

whoever said nature was kind
forgot the broken branches falling,
forgot the beating of silken wings
smashing against the wire.

wind

i see the wind as witness
to the inescapable
and to night
a voice so much
like no one's
and a coolness
so like yours

but not as cool
as the stone
you want to be
and will some day
become

country

i did not choose the place
so i could drink long glasses of cool shade,

and i did not sing your name
to change the water tadpoles into frogs;

i did not walk this field
to tell you you were only half alive,

but you have taken the grains
and spread them one by one along your arm.

nothing much can happen
without barley fields to finger in the last light

of dying july sun
or plangent yellow moon.

serpent

golden leaves glisten and return
to the sympathetic air
to the unfed ground.

sunshine spangles on the garden snake
deflects the eye abounding
to leaves and grass and scraps of fractured light.

pull back that stick
and do not strike the unbridled air,
the famished earth,

nor the golden snake
spangle buried and unbetrayed

face unlooking
tail unwavering
eyes of tiny stone unblinking.

north

eighteen hours to the north –
a path to unmapped terrain,
the vast and undiscovered province
we say is ours.

in a drive to the sault as interminable
as marriage is relentless.

eighteen years a mere drop
in the pledged scheme,
a death pact made in a crowded church.

perversity

i read in the news
to defeat global warming
the american army plans to invade the sun
they mean business
they will stay the course
they will not be deterred by naysayers
radicals, liberals, lefties
or being burned alive.

weeds between paving stones
students flunking english
and my love for you
are likewise perverse
and immune to failure.

meditation is a balcony
from which we view mind
cheering on defeat:
a frog explodes in
slowly boiling water
but thrown in suddenly
it will venture a jailbreak
and recreation.

floorboards

back of a cupboard under the floor
are your scimitar and your lute,

you are afraid to wield them;
both are circuits to sadness.

anyone proclaiming grief's mess
would marvel at the tidiness of yours

kept under the creaky floorboards
in a jewel-encrusted box

with mother-of-pearl inlay.
in your mind you finger

and count every burning shekel
while never opening the box.

oracles

indwelling

intend no other aim than silence
(so hard and worthy a plan)
bone simple.

to hold still inside a bubble
to let water surround a corpus floating,
do not steal the breath of indwelling
or the sparse glow of peace.

be the bright and tranquil yolk
inside an egg,
a birch leaf wayward floating
on a languid oval pond.

pattern only the still droplet
in a cool cistern,
empty tankard
or stolen chalice

for if a moment could be garnered
strange would be the lull.

marrakech

the medina teems with antics,
souks and mules press against us,
tajines and sheep heads sizzle
in an unreal light.

jars of live scorpions are sold –
some come with their own exorcist.

fire eaters, dancers and magicians
throw us through the streets like flames.
i am lost in the hungering.

if we take some of your mint tea
sweetened to excess,
will you let us go,
release us to the palmerie?

or free us to the desert?
there scorpions are not jarred.
the wild cradled dunes
are magician and exorcist.

majorelle garden

bamboo, bougainvillea, geranium,
laurel, hibiscus and cypress,
four hundred kinds of palm trees
and two thousand cacti,
water lilies in a pool of papyrus.

we fell in love with morocco
as jacques majorelle did in 1923.
we weren't tubercular,
were not painters (exactly),
and didn't stay for decades.

nonetheless
we found a garden,
revelled in intense light.

a splendid moorish villa, bou safsaf,
in tones of deep blue, green and red,
an art deco studio with perglos and blue walls
stood in tropical luxuriance,
fassi ceramics and berber doors
opening on the bright of mind.

if we could build this dome in air,
this art deco palace, engravings of marrakech
scratched onto our remembering,
these villages, kasbahs and souks,
sunny pleasure domes without ice,
we would inhabit a world of gardens.

southern oases

the draa valley hatched rulers and swords,
brought centuries vast as stony plains,
moroccan dynasties, almoravid, saadians and
alaouites,
were birthed from mountains and pre-saharan sands.

three rivers carved its gorges,
dizzying red cliffs sculpted from the sides
of high atlas and anti-atlas, distinct mountain ranges
moving away from each other through time,

while small plots of corn and barley below red and
yellow peaks
take gratefully what moisture they find.
hundreds of ancient kasbahs,
fortified pink villages,
in the groves of palm
and white almond-blossoming trees.

an ancient mosaic:
berber caucasian and craggy mountains
sub-saharan negro and desert sands
indigenous nomad and palmed oases
post-colonial arab and village farms
dwelt together centuries ago and now.

riad dar fakir

"Staying in a riad is usually an experience that will transport you to another time and place." (Eyewitness Guide to Morocco)

riad means garden.
ours has a rooftop terrace
a colourful courtyard
and not a single plant.

incense hangs heavy in the air
indian music is piped through speakers,
hindu gods peek from the shadows.
we're not expected to know
the difference between north africa and the far east.

natasha says she has a bad feeling.

a riad is a house with an enclosed garden.

there is no soil, but
the clients are ornately young
like the rugs and cushions layered
splashed with glitter and reds
and dark heavy walnut
intricate and carved by hand.

riad means garden;
there are no trees.

in islam the garden of eden is the beginning
(as in other faiths).
the hanging gardens of babylon
are an ancient wonder.

riad means garden,
yet there are no flowers.

the lighting is poor and
everything begins to unravel,
but i feel at home
in the plush plantless
riad, where a creature
of darkness can hide from the light.

mhamid

village boys of mhamid
mocked us as we passed,
we, delighted children at a carnival,
rode dromedaries

wore the saharwi headscarves
we were told to buy;

even the animals showed
a certain cynicism about us –
doubtless they suspected
no real need for camels.

contemptuous four-legged slaves
begged from us,
heads nuzzling up
for an orange peel or a stale croissant
bright sand reflecting their sycophancy
toward the tourist petty tyrant,
hot sun glaring on
the playtime of the rich.

sacred

stream alone in the desert,
its browns and greens receding,
a burble barely audible –

they saw only one stream,
a single oasis.

too full of desert,
they struggled with heat.

ibrahim placed an arm
on father's shoulder
and together they stared at water,
cut through the blazing,

barely sounding burble
of shared laughter.

the brook brought
human touch as holy trickle,
a swath through sacred thirst.

sahara

in the sahara there are two drinks
thirst and thirstier

and there is nothing
between a girl and
herself

not the sheltering sky with stars beyond stars
                                    numberless
not the golden silk bathing your walking feet
not the silver-black scaraba writing hieroglyphs
                                    across the dunes

brief worldly nomads
we longed to stay
with jamal who had us laugh at dromedaries
with anne-marie climbing the highest sands
with the saharwi man whose thin face spoke
of kindness and of thirst

the ancient script dissolved at night
invisible desert
unwatered page

the nomads' tents were made of chocolate cloth
and we slept soundly stretched out on the sands.

prophecy: 2

i took refuge
in the stolen land
on my way home.

angels appeared,
spheres revealed constellations
a braille to my blindness;
dream crystals fell,
were vanquished on the lake.

i felt i were seeing
things
i had no right to see
– sacred things.

i turned away, and
when i looked again,
the future was gone.

sun, pines and prophecy

beneath the pines splayed needles abound,
spiky to eye – yet unthinkably soft.
pine trees are visors for the sun,
no eyes should unite with such glare;
while skin welcomes the solar rays' caress
direct and unatoned.

in those fields she wanders
a cassandra cursed, deviant and prophetic.
vision and knowledge are merciless solar fire
piercing an eggshell retina.

let eyelids enfold and encrust
to grant a willing blindness,
to fulfil a mope-eyed, glare-resistant urge,
this time to unknow,
so an eyeless wanderer, purged of prophecy,
may stroke her body with sunlight and pine.

time

monstrous delusion
causing us to crumble
before the eyes:

eyes with whites
blues and browns –
vehicular and tragic.

would we be star-crossed
and obsessed if time's
mantle dropped?

if the clock stopped ticking
its funereal song,

and brought us fully
to our native noon.

to julian the magician

julian the magician, god of wonder
snakes, wands and swords!
take on our contemporary god –
an electrical wizard and genius of pyrotechnics.

invert the mechanical magic of this time and place,
this city whose pulse is a subway
whose heart a turbine.

bring forth the natural fibres of meaning
the silken scarves that turn to rabbits and sparrows,

crush the audience's wristwatch, great julian.
spit into the clay of time,
stitch the split atoms of being,
tie us into knots, pull eggs from our ears,
then turn our cards and coins
back into doves and wishes.

chinese restaurant

a line of spruce trees
array the horizon,
the strip mall's forgotten ancestors.

sipping jasmine tea,
one cheek facing a solar-sinking west,
i read the placemat horoscopes
and downturned january faces
of parking lot people.

i was without money to pay for tea;
mrs. guy said it was fine
and beamed on my other cheek
with a smile eastward rising.
the wood ancestors stood still –
the world was bigger than i knew.

votive candles in cathedrals

fire can burst forth
from words or
breath
or other worlds;

but this large collection
of candles
undercuts fire

– heat so temporary,
subject to fire codes
and metal containers.

perhaps a child is a
match.
she ignites something
rare

leibnizian universes
spinning
ablaze in the darkness.

the woman with the empty bowl

she has an empty bowl
made of wood and lacquer;

she sits waiting by the door
marked with the number zero in white paint

and she knows something
you do not yet know,

nor perhaps ever shall:

that the bowl cannot contain things put in it,
and the door will remain a door
whether opened or shut,

that the number could be any other
and would still signify none,

that hands are empty bowls
even as they clasp.

word

earthbound

gravity loves the body
as flesh adores the earth.

if words were grapes,
pulp and juice, to suck and swallow,
i would pick them.
if language were hammock to lift and turn in
i'd lie in it awhile.
if paragraphs were boats for hovering over space,
i would ride always.

blood and bones cleave to matter.
arms want arms, not sentences,
hands need hands, not phrases to hold.
inside there is a hunger for food and drink and sleep;
movement is my story;
sleep my only poem.

listen

"Listen, too,
How every pause is filled with under-notes,
Clear, silver, icy, keen awakening tones
Which pierce the sense and live within the soul."
(P. B. Shelley)

pauses are fuller
than sounds,

lethe is replete
with dreams,

a lost mandolin or flute
is enough.

we have known
the space was our time:

the past which is always here
the here which is only the past.

play on your flute, the silences
between the tones –

those feelings that were lost
but still dwell in the small crevices

of time.
those silences,

each of those spaces is
my daughter, sister, lover

and they are openings, breaths,
between the words and sounds.

ineffable

for this she was hanged
on the semblance of love,
a rood, a bare cross,
and awaited our birth;

she is the dung beetle,
the scarab of new life –
not tidy or sweet.

she is the grass of november,
a sarcophagal spot of time.
she is prolific and devouring:
cancer of the body, and
dark night of the soul.

desire took the salt out of her blood,
wasted her –
a hollow husk that once held corn.
kiss her wounds,
each second of life is a reckoning
she is the pagan christ.

tin drums

tin drums are sounding -
a suppliant palm on a resonant hand
plays a memorable beat.

a hollow murmur
percussive yet weak;
a mild tap will echo
so much and so little.

desire has nowhere to flow,
runs askew in odd places,
(store flyers and malls) because
if a leak is stopped, another bursts forth.

ours is an old hose
an ancient pipe or wire,
while life is a tin drum sounding
on tentative hands.

spatial poetics and the message of the pebble

such deftness unfolds words
usual and unusual

gliding along the page
of synapses

saying what was partly
understood or necessary.

for wind is muse
when mixed with a liberal dose of language,

when it shakes and scatters
the spruce needles, twirling maple seeds

into the pool
unconscious and therefore real.

on the slow walk to the mailbox
i never wear shoes

pebbles interject between
toes to remind me

poems are like both pebbles and breezes,
but more like walking than shoes.

tangible words

i waited a long time
but words came when i was busy,
so they were forgotten
left as usual on the counter.

in the morning they were sprawled about the room
not paper or ink
just some disembodied poems.

their timing was terrible.
they almost upset the tea
they fell into the cream.

i took them out and shook them off,
but i didn't know where to put them.
the closets and cupboards were all full
so i stuffed them in our junk drawer
- the back of my head.

later they fell out;
i tidied them away again –
i didn't want the guests
to see them lying about
the empty cups, the dust
balls and my unwritten poems.

activist shopping

a polemical catalogue:
buttons, posters and t-shirts
proclaim *organic cotton*
and *renewable agriculture*.

i cannot dispute
al gore rocks,
and so i buy a compact disc of
"lullabies from the axis of evil,"
tack the radical alphabet to our wall:
a is for africa,
c is for choice,
w is for witch.

i feel wistful for
the lost alphabet
of naïve apple,
innocent cat
and simple red wagon.

the hillsides are so littered with loveliness,
the red earth is touched with footprints
while words flutter,
pale moths against the light.

blake: 445f

1

the teacher spoke
to the marriage of all things,
to the breaking of chains.

"the good guys are naked.
the bad guys are clothed,"
she told them.

one with twinkling eyes
said the class should be naked.

"yes, in a course on blake,
clothing is perverse," she laughed.

2

she spent the week in worry
that some brave soul would do it,
would come to class stark naked,
fulfill the prophet's words,
break all their chains
and set the orbs to spinning;
so she fretted
saw herself in headlines –
the prof who told students to come
naked as the day they were born.
her good name tarred and feathered,
condemned and unemployed.

3

the class met under the ancient trees.
sun sequins touched their hair, their eyes,
and she was oddly grieved
to see them fully clothed
so far away from their day of birth.
not a towel or toga or bathing suit
to challenge that dull round.

4

and so once again
the garden becomes a desert
we are cast out from Eden.
the sun and stars stay in their orbit;
apocalypse breathes on its edges faintly
unearthly shame trembles over the bleached bones,
curbing imagination
and its sacred human form.

bog poem

i would rather fail at this task
than succeed at any other
digging peat
from the bog

it nourishes me –
this burrowing, trenching, cutting,
to blink dazed into the day after
staring blank
for untold hours
at the dark waterlogged wood.

this peat will give light to someone,
who doesn't know or care
this digging and wedging
cost the earth and
warmth comes
from its blackened soot.

writing

the pen left the page
fell asleep in a drawer
and left those marks
black on white
furled wings against a page of sky.

while you and it met in slumber
flecks birdlike straddled the horizon
billowing on waves of air.

dolls play when people leave the room.
while you sleep
words cull the fluid of your mind
becoming birds
cutting through the clouds
reaching to the sun.

notes

child on jebel toubkal: Jebel Toubkal (Mount Toubkal) is the highest mountain in North Africa.

middle cove is near St. John's, Newfoundland.

hrothgar takes its title character, a King of Denmark, from the Anglo Saxon poem, *Beowulf.*

perversity adopts the phrase "ventures: a jail-break and re-creation" from Margaret Avison's "Snow". It also alludes to Al Gore's "An Inconvenient Truth" in the metaphor of the frog exploding in slowly boiling water.

to julian the magician: Julian the Magician is a character from Gwendolyn MacEwen.

listen begins with a quotation from Shelley's *Prometheus Unbound* (4.1.188-91).

spatial poetics and the message of the pebble was inspired by the poetry of Don McKay.

blake 445f alludes to a number of Blake poems, including *The Marriage of Heaven and Hell, The Mental Traveller,* and *Milton.*

bog poem was influenced by my reading of Seamus Heaney's many beautiful bog poems and a visit to Ireland.